sundance
publishing

LITTLE RED
READERS

Places I Like

PETER SLOAN &
SHERYL SLOAN

This is a mountain.
I like mountains.

This is a beach.
I like beaches.

This is a forest.
I like forests.

This is a lake.
I like lakes.

This is a desert.
I like deserts.

This is a river.
I like rivers.

This is a city.
I like cities.